MANAGING COSTS, TIPS & SUMMARY

INFO YOU MUST KNOW!

- Regularly comparing "actual" vs. "estimated" costs is important in keeping any job on track and profitable.
- Such costs comparisons are possible only when you have a schedule, necessary resources and corresponding timeframes.

ESTIMATED VS. ACTUAL COSTS

Estimated Costs

- Estimated cost are quantitative assessments of the likely costs of the resources required to complete project activities.
  Note: Estimated costs may be presented in summary or in detail.
- Cost estimates are generally expressed in units of currency (dollars) in order to facilitate comparisons both within and across projects. Other units such as hours or days may be used.
  Note: In some cases, estimates are provided using multiple units of measure to facilitate appropriate management control.

Actual Costs

- The actual cost (AC) of a project represents the true total and final costs accrued during the process of completing all work during the pre-determined period of time allocated for all schedule activities as well as for all work breakdown structured components.
- Actual costs are primarily made up of a number of specific items including, but not limited to, cost in direct labor hours, direct costs alone, and also all costs including indirect costs.
  Note: Actual costs should be thoroughly itemized in detail throughout the project.

RESOURCE ALLOCATING & LEVELING

- Cost/Resource allocation (or loading): Resources in this context include: labor, equipment and materials.
- Cost loading is assigning the appropriate cost (or budget) to each activity.
- When the cost of all activities are added up, the total should be equal to the project's budget.
- Resource allocation, means assigning the right amount of resources to each activity at the right time.
- The objective of this step is to load each activity with the amount of resources it requires and calculate its budget.

RULES & TIPS FOR PLANNING

- All tasks must have markers that enable everyone to tell that the work is actually complete.
- Avoid micro planning.
- Construct the schedule on paper first.
- You must know both cost and schedule to know where your project actually is.
- The overall shutdown time is usually critical in jobs that require a lengthy period of down-time.
- There is nothing more damaging to planning and project management than missed start-up times.
- Remember that some activities are independent of others but some must happen simultaneously.

PROJECT MANAGER/ SCHEDULER – SUMMARY

The successful project manager/scheduler should be prepared to do the following:

- Be able to read plans and measure them accurately.
- Possess a fair knowledge of arithmetic, together with the knowledge of English and metric systems.
- Be able to visualize (draw a mental picture) of the building from the plans.
- Have an intimate knowledge of the job conditions, most practical methods of handling materials and labor on the job.
- Have the knowledge and ability to assemble materials into workable units.
- Possess an intimate knowledge of labor performances and operations and convert them into dollars and cents.
- Avoid labor disputes caused by inadvertent violation of labor union contracts.
  Work by certain trades may be different in various states.
- The successful project manager should foresee cost over-run on the project by creating and monitoring the S-curve and Bell Curve charts.

GLOSSARY

A/E: Architect/Engineer, usually the designer of the project hired by the Owner.
Activities: tasks/work done workers or subcontractors.
Arrow Diagram: Flow chart with arrows and event nodes.
As-Built Plans: approved plans, which show all revisions and changes.
BOCA: Building Officials and Code Administrators International, Inc.
Building Permit: Authorization required by local government for new buildings or major alteration
Calendar Days: Actual days of the week in place of working days.
Certification of Occupancy: Official notification by building department that job is complete.
Change of Scope: revision to original contract
Change order: written revisions to contract
Civil Engineer: a professional registered in the state to practice in the field of civil works.
Class A: General Engineering Contractor who builds civil works like roads, bridges and dams, usually hired by the governmental agency.
Class B: General Building Contractor, who builds residential, commercial and industrial structures, usually hired by the owner.
Class C: Specialty Contractor includes Plumbing, Electrical, HVAC, etc. Usually hired by the General Building Contractor.
Cleanup: Housekeeping done by subcontractors after work.
Composite crew: a building team made up of laborers, journeymen and foremen for certain trades.
Contingency: An event that may occur affecting cost or time.
CPM: Critical Path Method
Craft: A trade occupation requiring skill and training
Direct Cost: costs of all permanently installed materials and equipment and the labor required.
Drawings: Plans & specifications prepared by architect/ engineer and approved by building department.
Dummy Arrow: Line without time or work, indicates only a sequence of restraints without activity.
Early start: work beginning before scheduled time
Earthwork: Excavation, fill, compaction and grading
Electronic Surveying: Field measurements made by electronic or laser instruments.
Event Numbering: Identification of an activity
Events: See activities
Extras: Cost in excess of that given in contract
Float or free time: amount of time any given activity can be delayed.
Foundations: concrete or masonry work that supports building or structure.
General Conditions: See indirect costs
General contractor: One who contracts for the construction of an entire building.
Grading: Modification of ground to conform to plans
Grub: to remove tree roots
HVAC: Heating-Ventilating Air Conditioning
ICBO: International Conference of Building Officials
ICC: International Code Council
Incidental Time Items: Start-up and wind down time, supervisory instructions, maintenance and clean-up work area during and end of shift, tool box meetings, unloading and transporting materials getting tools and equipment.
Indirect Costs: All costs other than direct costs that do not become a permanent part of the project.
Indirect Field Costs: See indirect cost
Inspections: required inspections by local codes
Job overhead: see indirect costs
Lead-time: amount of time required between ordering and delivery of material or equipment
Main account: sitework, concrete, masonry, misc. steel, rough and finish carpentry, moisture protection, doors and windows, finishes, specialties, mechanical and electrical.
Employee-hour: labor time expended per person per hour
Pavement: concrete or asphalt slab
Permits: government authorization for construction, plumbing, electrical work, etc.
PERT: Program Evaluation and review technique
Plumbing: work connected with water and wastewater
Portmortem: an evaluation and documentation of entire project from initial through completion, or completions vs. schedule and cost vs. estimate.
Project Closeout Activities: Disconnecting temporary electrical and water services and removing signs
Reinforcement: Steel bars and wire mesh used in concrete or masonry.
Rough plumbing: concealed plumbing
Standard Labor Cost: Cost per employee-hour according to US Dept. Labor.
Standard Unit Employee-hours: time required for performing work under site conditions, familiarity and skill with work, proper supervision, adequate supply of workers, unobstructed access, temperatures between 40° and 85°, 40-hour week and 8 hour days.
Standard Unit Subcontract Price: Work done on a subcontract basis.
Start-up activities: obtaining permits, on-site sanitary facilities, lot survey, temporary electricity & water supply.
Surveying and Layout: Field measurement made by construction surveyor to locate foundations, set grades and establish property corners.
Testing: field test of soil and materials required by building Department.
Time phasing: time required for selecting cont[illegible] negotiation or bidding or time for executing w[illegible]
Total Float: Amount of time an activity can b[illegible] without adversely affecting overall time.
Unit Material Cost: cost for each bd-ft of lu[illegible] concrete, sf of paving.
Work Elements or Work Accounts: activities [illegible]s of each main account.

BUILDER'SBOOK,INC./BOOKSTORE&PUBLISHER Foradditionalcopies,afulllineofCodes,ReferenceBooks,Videosandotherresourcesrelatedtothistopic,call 1(800)273-7375or1(818)887-7828,orFax(818)887-7990orvisitthestoreatitsphysicaladdress8001CanogaAvenue,CanogaParkCA91304.orthewebsite:www.buildersbook.com.
COPYRIGHT/DISCLAIMER: Copyright2018Builder'sBook,Inc.Allrightsreserved.Informationisprovidedinasummarizedformtoprovideaquickguidetothissubjectmatter.The informationsummarizedhereinissubjecttochangebylegislativeandregulatoryaction,withoutnotice.Thisquickguideisbynomeansintendedtobecomprehensivenorauthoritative. Consultoriginalcodesourcesand/orcompetentprofessionalsforguidanceonyourspecificsituation.Thepublisherisnotprovidinglegal,accounting,orotherprofessionalservicesandis not liable for any damage, however caused, resulting from the use or reliance on the information presented in this card. website: www.buildersbook.com.
ISBN - 13: 9[illegible]06 - 3
ISBN - 10: [illegible]
9781622701063
U.S. $8.95
T2-BRL-257

PROJECT MANAGEMENT SCHEDULING
RESIDENTIAL & COMMERCIAL

QUICK-CARDS® *A Unique Quick-Reference Guide*

80[illegible]
1-8[illegible]
D0129206

PROJECT MANAGEMENT & SCHEDULING – INT[illegible]

INFO YOU MUST KNOW!

Planning and scheduling are two terms that are often thought of as synonymous, but they are not.

- Scheduling is just one part of planning. It is the determination of the timing and sequence of operations.

PROJECT SCHEDULER – 3 TYPES OF KNOWLEDGE

A scheduler must have 3 types of knowledge:

- Knowledge of computer software
- Knowledge of principles of scheduling and project control
- Knowledge of specific technical field of the project.

JOB SCHEDULE

- Match the type of scheduling tool to the job at hand.
- Smaller jobs may only need a simple bar chart and activity list.
- Larger, more complex projects, may need computerized systems.
- A schedule must:
  - List each activity
  - Estimate time needed for each activity.
  - Specify the who, what, where & when for each task.
  - Include start-up activities that must be completed before construction begins, such as drawings and permits, utility hookups, on-site sanitary facilities and locating lot corners.
- Scheduling a project requires an understanding of all the individual units of work required.
- See Activity Lists section of this Quick-Card.

PROJECT MANAGER & SCHEDULER

- The responsibility of maintaining the schedule must be given to the project manager superintendent and forepersons.
- An effective project manager coordinates the work of various trades and ensures that each activity is started and completed on time.
- The schedule should include all code-required inspections at specified points during construction– such as foundations, framing, plumbing, electrical, final inspection and client walk-though. If any inspection is over-looked, the next phase of work can be delayed.
- The scheduler must ensure that all materials are available when they are needed, by ordering well in advance.
- The scheduler must give all vendors and subcontractors sufficient advance notice.
- Provide important schedule information and regular updates to suppliers, employees, subcontractors, lenders and customers.

MANAGING PROJECT COMMUNICATION – 4 PROCESSES

1. **Communication Planning.** Determine who needs what information, how frequently they need it and how it will be given to them.
2. **Information Distribution.** The process of making needed information available to those who need it in a timely manner.
3. **Performance Reporting.** Collecting and distributing information on progress; this includes measuring progress, reporting status and forecasting future results.
4. **Administrative Closure.** This includes gathering information and generating and disseminating information about a phase or final project closeout.

MASTER ACTIVITY LISTS FOR RESIDENTIAL & COMMERCIAL JOBS

MASTER ACTIVITY LISTS

The master activity lists shown here can help improve your accuracy and reduce the time required to produce a schedule. These lists contain all the typical activities in residential and commercial projects. Grouping activities by project phase (as shown here) helps organize them into a usable list.

ACTIVITY LIST FOR RESIDENTIAL JOBS

PROJECT START UP
- Obtain a permit
- Obtain approved drawings
- Obtain plot of site
- Temp. power and water
- Builder's Risk Insurance
- Surveyor locates corners

OWNER ACTIVITIES
- Select plumbing fixtures
- Select light fixtures
- Select HVAC system
- Select paint
- Select cabinets

INITIAL SITEWORK
- Clear and grade site

FOUNDATION PHASE
- Set batter boards
- Dig footings
- Set grade stakes
- Footing inspection
- Pour piers and footings

SLAB PREP WORK
- Fine grade sub-base
- Set batter boards
- Place wire mesh
- Set grade stakes
- Set UG pipe and conduit

PLACE SLAB
- Place and finish concrete
- Cure concrete

WOOD FRAME PHASE
- Order framing material
- Deliver framing material
- Erect floor framing, walls and sheathing
- Deliver roof trusses
- Install roof framing
- Complete rough framing
- Check plumb and square
- Check door openings
- Install wall insulation
- Framing inspection
- Clean up waste material

UTILITY ROUGH-IN
- Deliver tubs and showers
- Plumbing top-out
- Plumbing inspection
- HVAC and elect rough-in
- Electrical inspection

FRAME CLOSE-IN PHASE
- Install sheathing and exterior wood items

EXTERIOR MASONRY
- Order brick
- Deliver brick
- Install veneer and chimney

ROOFING ITEMS
- Install shingles, install flashing and felt

FINISH PHASE
- Interior wall material
- Wall finish items
- Paint interior walls
- Paint exterior walls
- Deliver wallpaper
- Hang wallpaper
- Paint or stain interior trim
- Paint or stain doors
- Paint touch-up

INTERIOR WOOD TRIM
- Deliver interior trim
- Install interior trim
- Install shelving and rods
- Install interior doors

FINISH FLOORING
- Install ceramic tile
- Install other hard tile
- Install vinyl tile
- Install carpet

INSTALL MISC. ITEMS
- Insulate attic
- Order cabinets
- Deliver cabinets
- Install cabinets
- Install bathroom accessories
- Order appliances
- Deliver and set appliances
- Install brick
- Install stove
- Install compactor
- Install washer/dryer
- Install range hood

FINISH UTILITIES
- Plumbing trim-out
- HVAC trim-out
- Deliver HVAC equipment
- Set grills and thermostat
- Start up and test equipment

ELECTRICAL TRIM-OUT
- Hook up main power
- Check and test system
- Final electrical inspection

CUSTOM ITEMS
- Install fireplace items
- Install outside decks
- Install hot tubs
- Install alarm systems
- Install telephone wiring
- Install TV wiring

FINISH SITEWORK
- Grade driveway and walks
- Install concrete driveway
- Form and place sidewalks
- Site landscaping

CLOSE-OUT PHASE
- Disconnect temporary utilities
- Clean house
- Final inspection

ACTIVITY LIST FOR COMMERCIAL JOBS

PROJECT START UP
- Obtain a permit
- Obtain approved drawings
- Obtain plot of site
- Temporary power and water
- Builder's Risk Insurance

INITIAL SITEWORK
- Clear and grade site
- Surveyor locates corners of lot & building

EARTHWORK
- Excavation basement
- Backfill

FOUNDATION PHASE
- Piles and caissons
- Set rebars and wire mesh
- Spread and continue footings
- Column pedestals
- Grade beams
- Fdn inspection

SLAB PREP WORK
- Fine grade sub-base
- Set batter boards
- Place rebar and wire mesh
- Set grade stakes
- Place UG pipe and conduit

MASONRY
- Rebars
- Basement walls

PLACE SLABS
- Place and finish concrete
- Cure concrete

STEEL FRAME PHASE
- Order framing material
- Deliver framing material
- Erect cols, floors & wall framing
- Deliver roof-framing materials
- Install roof framing
- Check plumb and square

MISC. IRON & PARTITIONS
- Steel bar joists & decking
- Place floor slabs
- Install interior walls
- Install door frames
- Install wall insulation
- Framing inspection
- Clean up waste material

UTILITY ROUGH-IN
- Deliver plumbing fixtures
- Plumbing top out
- Rough in HVAC & electrical
- Install fire sprinkler system
- Electrical inspection

FRAME CLOSE-IN PHASE
- Install exterior curtain walls
- Install exterior windows

ROOFING ITEMS
- Install roofing
- Install sheetmetal
- Install roof drains

FIREPROOFING PHASE
- Fireproof steel columns
- Fireproof steel beams

FINISH PHASE
- Wall finish items
- Lath and plaster
- Paint interior walls
- Paint or stain doors
- Paint touch-up

INTERIOR WOOD TRIM
- Install interior trim
- Install interior doors

FINISH FLOORING
- Install ceramic tile
- Install other hard tile
- Install vinyl tile
- Install carpet
- Install wood flooring
- Install misc. items
- Install restroom items

FINISH UTILITIES
- Plumbing trim-out
- HVAC trim-out
- Set grills and thermostat
- Start up and test equipment
- Fire sprinkler system
- Electrical trim-out
- Hook up main power
- Check and test system
- Final electrical inspection

CUSTOM ITEMS
- Install fire alarm system
- Install telephone wiring
- Install TV wiring
- Elevator and electrical stairs
- Metal toilet stalls

FINISH SITEWORK
- Storm & sanitary sewers
- Grade driveway and walks
- Install concrete driveway
- Form and place sidewalks
- Site landscape

CLOSE-OUT PHASE
- Disconnect temporary utilities
- Clean building site
- Final inspection

© 2019 Builder's Book, Inc. All rights reserved.

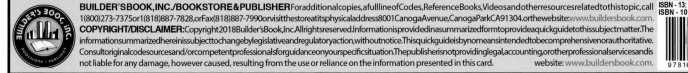

BAR CHARTS

- A bar chart shows the sequential relationship between various activities and how they fit together in a project.
- The chart indicates the date of the beginning and the date of completion of each unit of operation.
- Activities that will be performed to accomplish the job are listed in the left column.
- The time required to perform each step is indicated in the columns to the right of the left column.
- These steps are listed in sequence for each element of work.

The Bar Chart provides the scheduler a simple means of:
- Determining overall time required to complete the work through the use of a logical method.
- Determining the earliest time an activity can start and the latest time an activity can be completed without delaying the project completion.
- Determining the leeway, or free float, available for scheduling an activity.
- Reviewing each phase of the job in detail to make sure that the items such as special material and equipment are covered.
- Coordinating requirement between crafts.
- Comparing alternate methods for performing the job.

BAR CHARTS – FREE FLOAT & TOTAL FLOAT

- Free-float is the amount of time any activity can be delayed without adversely affecting the early start of any following activity. In other words, it's the difference between the earliest possible finish of a given activity and the early start of the following.
- Total float is the amount of time that an activity can be delayed without affecting the overall project completion.

INFO YOU MUST KNOW!
- Lead-times can range from less than an hour to several months.
- Missed start-up times are the most damaging to planning and project management.

BAR CHART SCHEDULING – RESIDENTIAL PRE-CONSTRUCTION SCHEDULE

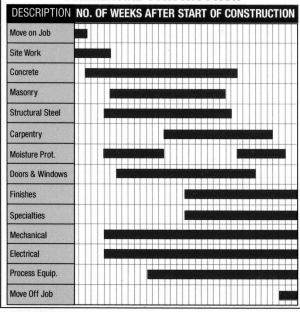

Bar Chart Scheduling Table

ID	Task Name	Duration	Start	Finish
1	Pre-Construction Prep	22.5 days	Mon 04/21/14	Wed 5/21/14
2	Obtain Zoning info/covenants	0 days	Mon 04/21/14	Mon 04/21/14
3	Supply lot sale agreement	0 days	Mon 04/21/14	Mon 04/21/14
4	Supply house plans	0 days	Mon 04/21/14	Mon 04/21/14
5	Engineering Structural/Soils	6 days	Mon 04/21/14	Mon 4/28/14
6	Apply for building permit	14 days	Tue 4/29/14	Fri 5/16/14
7	Create Construction bid docs	4 days	Tue 4/29/14	Fri 5/2/14
8	Dist. construction docs for bids	1.5 days	Tue 5/6/14	Tue 5/6/14
9	Bidding period	8 days	Tue 5/6/14	Fri 5/16/14
10	Bid deadline	0 days	Fri 5/16/14	Fri 5/16/14
11	Notify winning bidders	4 hrs.	Fri 5/16/14	Fri 5/16/14
12	Sign subcontractor agreements	1.5 days	Mon 5/19/14	Tue 5/20/14
13	Secure long-term financing	10 days	Mon 4/21/14	Fri 5/2/14
14	Secure construction loan	10 days	Mon 5/5/14	Fri 5/16/14
15	Begin Construction on site	1 day	Tue 5/20/14	Wed 5/21/14

ADVANTAGES OF BAR CHARTS

- It's simple. No complicated calculations are involved.
- Easy to prepare. Can be prepared anywhere with just a pencil and paper.
- Easy to understand. No technical or mathematical background needed.
- Time-scaled. The length of a bar representing an activity is proportional to its duration.
- Great for general planning
- Can serve as a basis for other, more complex schedules, like the Critical Path Method.

DISADVANTAGES OF BAR CHARTS

- Lack of logical representation. Does not answer the "why" of an activity's start date.
- Does not show the complex interdependence of activities in a project. Ex. some activities happen simultaneously.
- Size and complexity of project interferes with the simplicity of bar charts if the project is long or complex. However, bar charts can still be used in long and/or complex projects if used to:
  - show a subset of the work activities to maintain the simplicity of the bar chart.
  - show summary bars to maintain the simplicity of the bar chart.

BAR CHART SCHEDULING – COMMERCIAL CONSTRUCTION

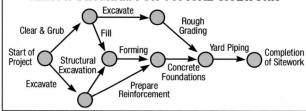

DESCRIPTION — NO. OF WEEKS AFTER START OF CONSTRUCTION

Move on Job
Site Work
Concrete
Masonry
Structural Steel
Carpentry
Moisture Prot.
Doors & Windows
Finishes
Specialties
Mechanical
Electrical
Process Equip.
Move Off Job

READING ARROW DIAGRAMS

- Arrow diagrams incorporate data from the bar chart and use arrows to link the activities.
- The tail of each arrow represents the start of the element; the head represents the finish.
- The length of the longest path through the diagram equals the total path required to complete the project.
- Shorter paths include arrows that indicate activities that may be performed simultaneously.
- Every element on the longest path is critical. Delay in one of these activities delays the project.
- An element on a shorter path is non-critical.
- Relationships among the activities are positioned in terms of precedence. Most activities have predecessor activities (activities that must be completed before the given activity can begin).
- Subsequent activities are those items that cannot begin until some prior activity is completed.
- Understanding the relationships between activities can provide greater flexibility and help better manage a schedule.

PROJECT PLANNING

- A project is initially planned without factoring time or availability of resources.
- Project planning consists of analyzing the project, breaking it into working elements and arranging these elements in an Arrow Diagram.
- The arrow diagram becomes the working model of the project.

ADVANTAGES OF ARROW DIAGRAMS

- Shows logical representation.
- Better than bar charts at representing large and complicated projects.

DISADVANTAGES OF ARROW DIAGRAMS

- Not time-scaled.
- Requires knowledge of how arrow diagrams work to produce them and understand them.

ARROW DIAGRAM FOR TYPICAL SITEWORK

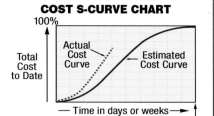

STRUCTURING ARROW DIAGRAMS

To structure an arrow diagram, the scheduler must analyze each activity and determine:
- What activity must immediately precede this element?
- What activity must immediately follow this element?
- What other activity, if any can be done simultaneously with this element?

INFO YOU MUST KNOW!
- The length of the arrow has no relation to the time it takes to do the job.
- All arrows may be about the same length, even though they represent jobs that take varying lengths of time.

CRITICAL PATH METHOD (CPM)

- The Critical Path Method or Critical Path Analysis is a mathematically based algorithm for scheduling a project.
- Commonly used with any project with interdependent activities.
- Calculates the longest path of planned activities to the end of the project.
- Calculates earliest and latest that each activity can start and finish without extending the project completion time.
- Determines "critical" activities (on the longest path)
- Prioritizes activities for the effective management and to shorten the planned critical path of a project by:
  - Pruning critical path activities
  - "Fast tracking" (performing more activities in parallel)
  - "Crashing the critical path" (shortening the durations of critical path activities by adding resources)
- On complex, long duration projects, a computer can process the date of the critical path system.
- In this method, final completion dates are continuously corrected as actual time is recorded.

Note: Maintenance of the chart can be a full-time job in itself, as there will be many changes on the job before it is finalized.

CPM REQUIREMENTS

The essential technique for using CPM is to construct a model of the project that includes the following:
- A list of all activities required to complete the project (Work Breakdown Structure).
- The time (duration) that each activity will take to complete.
- The dependencies between the activities.

CONSTRUCTION DELAYS

- Delayed completion, extended overhead and loss of productivity require a chronology of the job, CPM is useful in providing this.
- Delays result in losses and litigation.

READING CRITICAL PATH METHOD (CPM)

- The encircled letters indicate each unit of operation, activity or decision listed on the Bar Chart.
- The number between the circled tasks, nodes, indicates the estimated time for that activity.
- Numbers are usually given in units of days or weeks required to complete that activity.
- By adding the total elapsed time along each path, the longest path can be determined.
- The longest path is called the Critical Path.
- Any delay in the Critical Path would delay the entire project.

BASIC GROUND RULES FOR CPM

The basic ground rules of CPM are:
- Planning and scheduling are separate operations.
- Planning always comes first.
- The CPM and PERT systems are meant to maintain an optimum construction schedule.
- The CPM and PERT systems illustrate how changes or delays on any specific activity can cause an overall delay in the project.

CPM – SUPPLEMENTAL STEPS

1. Review and analyze the schedule
   - Review the logic and make sure that every activity has the correct predecessor.
   - Common errors to look for: wrong, missing or redundant relationship and logic loops.
2. Implement the schedule
   - Choose start and finish dates within the range of the calculated dates.
3. Monitor and control the schedule
   - Compare the baseline with what has actually been done.
   - Analyze any deviation (variance) from the baseline and take corrective actions.
4. Revise the database and record feedback
   - This is a continuous process.
   - Document project in a well-organized, easy to retrieve manner.
   - Record unusual events
   - Explain adjustments

TYPICAL CRITICAL PATH METHOD (CPM) DIAGRAM

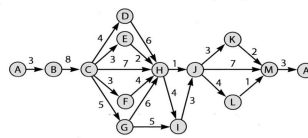

Circled letters represent events or completion of activity. Numbers between circles are estimated time periods for the completion of the activities.

CPM PREPARATION – 4 STEPS

Preparation for a CPM project includes the following 4 steps:

1. Determine the work activity
- Restrict the number of activities for the simplicity of the project schedule.
- Break the project down into small activities
- Factors considered in breaking down the project into individual activities:
  - Nature of work/homogeneity
  - Location/floor
  - Size/duration
  - Time Chronology
  - Responsibility
  - Phase

2. Determine the duration of activities. In most construction projects, durations are calculated in workdays, usually a 5-day workweek.
Duration = Total quantity / Crew productivity

3. Determine logical relationships
- A logical relationship exists between two activities, when the start (or finish) of one activity physically depends on the finish (or start) of another activity.
- The order of activities is determined by logical relationships. However, sometimes some activities are put before the others because of resource constraint (restriction).
- A resource constraint (or restriction) is when you can theoretically do two tasks at the same time, but you schedule one as a predecessor of the other because of resource (labor, equipment) limitation.

4. Draw the logic network and perform the CPM calculations
- The logic network and CPM can be done by hand however, there are computer programs that can accurately perform these calculations and give you the calculated finish date of the project, the critical path and the available float for all non-critical activities.

Note: If you use a computer program to make the calculations, check the input and the output. Don't solely rely on the computer program for the CPM.

COST S-CURVE CHART

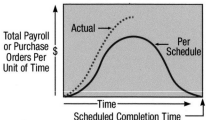

PROJECT ESTIMATING & S-CURVE

- Projects that are accurately estimated and completely managed follow a similar S-curve.
- The value of using this curve is that at half-way or three quarters through the project, it becomes clear whether the project is on track or heading for a loss. Corrective measures can be taken, and losses avoided or minimized.
- Ideally, the curve ends in the estimated total cost and time.

Note: If the curve ends at a total lower cost, the contractor makes more profit.
If the curve ends at a higher total cost, there is less profit, or worse, a loss.

S-CURVE

- S-curves are an important project management tool.
- S-curves allow the progress of a project to be tracked visually over time, and form a historical record of what has happened to date.
- Analyses of S-curves allow project managers to quickly identify project growth, slippage and potential problems that could adversely impact the project if no remedial action is taken.
- The S-curve shows, at any moment in time, the accumulated costs of the materials, subcontracts, labor and many other important aspects of the job.
- The chart consists of the summation of costs in dollars throughout the progress of work on a daily, weekly or monthly basis.
- The vertical scale of the chart is measured in dollars, employee-hours, or units of materials, in which the upper limit is the total estimated cost, employee-hours or material.
- The horizontal scale of the chart is measured in time.

S-CURVE PATTERN

- The first part of the curve rises at a gradual incline during the start-up period.
- As the job progresses and efficiency improves, the curve becomes steeper at a steady rate.
- Near the end of the project, the curve flattens again as fewer persons are employed and fewer/smaller material purchases are made.

BELL CURVE

- The bell curve is similar to the S-curve, except it shows the cost of material, subcontract or labor per week or per month.
- The bell curve normally grows slowly at the beginning of the job, increases during the bulk of the work and slows down at the end of the project.
- When actual spending varies from the bell curve, it's a warning that the job is running into trouble.
- The labor-power loading curve on a construction site over the duration of the construction schedule is typically an asymmetrical bell curve.

BELL CURVE CHART